Where Divinity Begins

Where Divinity Begins

POEMS BY
Deborah DeNicola

ALICE JAMES BOOKS
CAMBRIDGE, MASSACHUSETTS

Acknowledgments

Grateful acknowledgment is made to the following publications in which the following poems appeared:

The Antioch Review: "Matisse In Nice," copyright © 1992 by *The Antioch Review,* Inc., first appeared in the *The Antioch Review:* Vol. 50, No. 4, Fall 1992, reprinted by permission of the editors; *Calliope:* "The Gladiolas"; *Cimarron Review:* "The Physicist's Wife"; *Cotton Boll: The Atlanta Review:* "I Write To Write You"; *The Eloquent Edge, 15 Maine Women Writers:* "Toward The Red .Moon"; *Fiction International:* "Rainmakers"; *The Journal:* "Where Divinity Begins," "Like a God"; *Kennebec:* "Just Ten" (in an earlier draft titled "Humility and Kindness"); *North:* "Interlude"; *Louisville Review:* "Where I Was"; *Poetry Misceleny:* "The Furthest Point"; *Psychological Perspectives:* "The Tanning Salon"; *Second Glance:* "Self-Portrait In August: Letter To An Analyst"; *Sleeping With Dionysus:* "Awaiting Dionysus"; *Tamaqua:* "The Expulsion From Paradise," "How To Pray."

Several of these poems were collected in a chapbook entitled *Psyche Revisited* 1992 as the Winner of the 1991 *Embers* Chapbook Competition from Embers Press, Guilford, Connecticut. The poem "Rainmakers" appeared in a letterpress chapbook containing 16 poems entitled *Rainmakers* under the author's previously married name, Deborah Ward published by Coyote Love Press/Romulus Editions, Portland, Maine 1984.

The epigram preceding "The Future That Brought Her Here" is from *Before Recollection* by Ann Lauterbach © 1987 Princeton University Press.

The epigram preceding the poem "Where I Was" is from *The Promise of Light* by Richard Jackson © 1990 by Galvin Press.

The epigram after the title page and the one preceding the poem "Toward The Red Moon" are from *Life Supports* by William Bronk © 1982 by North Point Press.

The epigram preceding "I Write to Write You" is from *Poems of Paul Celan,* translated by Michael Hamburger, © 1972, 1980, 1988 by Michael Hamburger, reprinted by permission of Persea Books, Inc.

The epigram preceding the poem "Like A God" is from *The Collected Poems of Wallace Stevens* © 1981 by Alfred A. Knopf.

Alice James Books gratefully acknowledges support from the National Endowment for the Arts and from the Massachusetts Cultural council, a state agency whose funds are recommended by the Governor and appropriated by the State Legislature.

Cover and text design by Charles Casey Martin.
Cover art from the *Borders Series: Reach* by Julie S. Graham.

Alice James Books are published by the Alice James Poetry Cooperative, Inc. Alice James Books, 33 Richdale Ave., Cambridge, Massachusetts 02140.

for Justin

Contents

ACCIDENTAL HEART

~

We have carnal knowledge. Even the mind has carnal knowledge. This is a certainty.
—William Bronk

How to Pray

The Gladiolas

are poised like the women of Gauguin.
The orange saris of their blossoms, green
leotards of limb.

They know their moment.
Having swallowed the sun and wind

their bodies ride
a throb, a breath—though they've been

cut, transported and put into a vase
where darkness waits to drench
their severed ankles, to soothe

warmer at the knee—
until the whole cellular spine is saturated with sea

and their souls collapse
on the barge to another lifetime.

Oh, let them laugh like bells, like
xylophones with their orange
and open notes

on top of the dying
seconds in between.

They know the air is humid with fog.
They know the music around them in requiem.
They know the oxygen they weep will mother the world.

Seven Dolphins

I can't tell where the frail air fractures
into water but feel the tingling thrill
of huge and graceful mammals diving

off to starboard, their coal-blue coats,
smooth and flat like that of whales.
It's a landscape tinned in winter light,

laminated ice, a sky so green
and indistinct it seems like nothing
but horizon. And I remember seven dolphins

on TV
that January morning when I didn't believe
the anchorman who said they'd found

some shreds of cloth from the white spacesuits,
corroded scraps of silver metal zippers,
torn bootstraps, NASA's dross

along the beach. Then, during the ceremony
to honor the memory of the six dead astronauts
and a teacher from New Hampshire—

after the spruce wreaths were thrown in,
after the carnations and the prayers,
the blown kisses—

an unexpected arc of dolphins rose against
the aquarian conjunction of morning
suns. They streaked the liquid eye

deep, as bystanders, hushed, astonished
like me in my modest living room,
almost dropped to their knees.

Like A God

Music is feeling, then, not sound...
—Wallace Stevens

Hammering of silence. The world on mute

so that feeling *is music*
and the echoing density

throbs its same sorcery across your throat
when you gaze at the lute of his mouth.

He is speaking without sound. He is speaking to you
with lips you would make moist

in an instant of singing—
but the moment is decades long and suspended

like a drawn bridge.
You think, then, you have time
to adjust the blush of your persona,

time to shift the chamois hum across your shoulders,
a little dancing shrug. Time
to suck the round, full vowels of his words

into your lungs, translate them
into arias, respond— And you do
have, in the sifting isthmus of this moment,

time
to massage the image
emblazoned in your vision

like some pentecostal visitation of light—
This is the ring of eternity
you have been called and fallen into— A universe

of fuschia exclamation points,
dilating stars and half-notes,

elliptical adagios
revealing the shorn blossoms of a sigh, *a love*
condemned

to the shrouded mansions of fantasia, *love*
both classical and pagan—

never to be consummate,

therefore immortal
like a god.

The Expulsion from Paradise

Between the orange blossoms and the fig trees
an anorexic angel with xanthous wings
shoves Adam, pulling his gaze
from daisyish flowers, rubbing fire
from flexed pectoral to shoulder

as Eve looks over a little sheepishly,
already checking her own way out. The Lord,
left hanging and horizontal,
rolls the rainbowed whorl
of his anger around
the globe of the First World,
Eden—where half-hidden

in his own wings, the feminine
faces of classical fates
frown down into the garden

to wedge against the gate
the inexorable wheel of the couple's troubles.

In fourteen hundred something
Giovanni di Paolo didn't know
that his Siennese painting in tempera
and gold would splinter like a mosaic

which is how we contemplate it
from the second millennium—

no golden apples in sight, no suffering clouds
in the free will of blue skies,
just four black and spindly snakes.

Ah Eve, that double-braided curse
of curiosity and sunlight—

It was Eve
let go her legs

to show the ocean of gentian stamens,
pulsing lilies, pulsing lilacs.

And while they put on His consciousness
with the sunstroke of her fruit,
the already ancient future
of these dried oils had to shatter

because He wanted them
in a cracked canvas,
framed matter—

as he watched
their ejection parachute

and applauded the awkward
fall.

Matisse in Nice 1917–1930

Was it the shifting negligee
of breeze, or the silver scent
in the room that seduced Matisse
into shining the restless landscape
inside him here, in the Mediterranean
December: light was tame in the morning,

still innocent at noon, then arousing
like a Siamese cat, sprawled
and passionate by three o'clock—

I sense he was struck
by a coup de foudre, hardly unpacking
in the Hotel Beau Rivage, by habit drawing
a cigar, the room tilting with the movement
of the earth and the undulating Côte

d'Azure. It rained for weeks and
as his pigments brewed, he was
reduced to sketching his umbrella
in a slop jar. He must have dreamed

his brushes running the outlines
of the room until the golden lion
sizzled one day through the clouds,
and for the decade he would
reproduce the rising
waves and spinning prints
like random planet patterns.

A few years later, chez Un
Place Charles-Félix, he would
zoom into juxtapositions, gauzy
priscilla curtains, windblown
backdrops of cardboard, tacked
armfuls of fabric, blazing
fleur-de-lis on fleur-de-lis

and screens with Oriental Odalisques
flaring their harem pantaloons,

ballooning stage-sets where he led
the statuesque Henriette Darricarrère

into gardens of buzzing interiors,
the salt crystals carrying his colors,
his chambers lit by balconies,
both south and west, different
textures of the luminous,

the former, a lush splash of flashbulb
head-on, the latter, fluid
as a cocktail and Henriette
at the piano while the boys played
checkers on the checkered tablecloth.

Their jackets, identically striped,
the Persian diamond of the rug
trimming terracotta tiles,
one wall, peppered with minuscule flowers,
supporting two mandolins
as an alabaster goddess watches
without lowering her eyes.

He cooked this dizzy ratatouille in still-life—
stirring each drop of space
with natural jungle light

so that the deeper in we step
through petals of dahlias and gardenias,
the more we bask in his busy obsession,
the sunny studio
within the canvas
until the light recedes
to the figure of a mortar jar,
a common bowl of lemons,
the faces of anemones
germinating new forms

within the black,
oval mirror.

The Pleasures of Schnapps

Driving the Susquehanna
through Pittston, Pennsylvania
to attend a friend's wedding,
we would be late—lost twice
in the hard rain, giving up,
we stopped at a truckers' roadside bar,
shot two games of pool
and drank Schnapps.

Because I had never drunk it
and wondered what it was,
he ordered four shots with chasers of beer.

And from the damp perfume of my past,
I unraveled my conscience
out the one dismal window,
left a trail without regret
to his first MG, the black one,
I christened *Swanny*
when both country stations
crooned the same steel tremolo at once.

She was parked out back.
Her frayed canvas roof
a bitten canape of caviar,
the torn veil of a deserted bride.

That night for the first time
I thought of marrying him. I slipped
into my shocking pink dress
and black patent heels
in the Ladies Room
of the Shell Station.

I was loose on a road map
with a man braver than day—
But I was too young
to be dressed in reckless pink, white
leather gloves and fluid stockings.

Too young to be ruined
by the feverish Schnapps
of any promising young man—

We swam in a giddy neon then—
That bittersweet peppermint extract
distilled to slip down the throat
like the first clandestine romance.

Where Divinity Begins

We wait till we're rendered inoperable. There's a hedge
almost impossible to crawl through, a thicket

of years, the same turf quick-sanding
beneath our clumsy feet. Only as a bumbling hero

in an effete Biblical tale
does one draw the sword and bring down Jericho.

Only on some driven and gifted god
can we model ourselves, lift

our evening goblets into the sundown's
wondrous accomplishments

and drink in the myth of the happy ending.
Failure translates to *again*

and how else does one become
different than, more

than before? What risk there is
is always there, dropping like fate,

the lack of choice, a smoky lens,
a choice

through which we've recognized all along,
our enemies in the mirror, their voices, old roses,

pressed between the pages of our ears,
all a roar like an ocean—

I say *Move*
through the depths of your overgrown country

like the god you'll never be
but some weak resemblance of—

Though inside you
ravens will howl,

lacerating air with their
serrated wings— Who knows,

without the infernal gnashing of teeth
where divinity begins?

How to Pray

Softly at first. Like a peony
drugged in her own concoction of dizzy light,
emitting a steady aroma into the drone
of the late summer bees.
Then with the languor of autumn

leaves, that yawn into yellow, bowing your head
like a dying aster, each erect blue star,
a vibrating tine
finding the OHM of the cosmos
tuned to the blue rain, your voice—

rich as the splashy evening dress
on its stolen hotel hanger,
each lamé eyelid, a haloed shower of gold
and the night in the window,
those velvet folds, ululating chaos.

Then as the skin on the knees winces louder,
you're grappling visibly
with the minted coining of words,
sounding your nouns with their open vowels
propelled by feverish verbs—

And finally, on your feet, at an earthshaking pitch,
shouting the clouds into laurels, webbing
the haunted heavens, priding yourself on the sheer
lusciousness of your raw supplications

for shelter, sustenance, love
no pain-making god in his good mind could resist.

The Passion of Emily

Abelard & Heloise

Because he could count how many angels
danced on the head of a pin. Because

when he spoke, clouds dispersed
and trees grew from his words.

Because the old Bishops blessed him
with the mantles of young men's minds

and when he taught, ballooning his Pied Piper's cape,
mesmerized students trailing behind him

like birds of some medieval Jesus,
the Law proclaimed he must be chaste.

～

In twelfth century France, lust
was fingered with scarlet gloves
in a cellar of the sacristy,
and cast out like any common demon.

But love was of a different order. Impossible
to amputate its crucifix, desire
inextricable as sin,
solid as a stake driven
through the heart and Heloise

impaled on him
in his thoughts night and day,
so that when he was invited
by the Canon, her uncle,
to lodge with them, temptation

in all its naked compulsion
was not even Socratic
argument.

And when she came to him
for her studies

and their minds
grappled on the mattress of fantasy, electrified

discourse danced—alchemical metals
conjuncted Venus or the moon

fallen into the straw barn
singeing the air with its astral ocean—

⁓

It was inevitable
the stable girl would find them
en flagrante delicto

and after fondling herself, after blackmail,
after eventually divulging all—
in the wintry dark of a saturnine night,
they would come

on the Canon's orders
to castrate him, staining the wood
of his rented room
with his bleeding testicles.

The flames of his screams
would wake Heloise in the other city
to which she fled
with child. In the dark of her wild longing

she'd renounce motherhood and join the convent,
go on loving Abelard as if he were God.

⁓

Over twenty years as a monk,
he could visit her on occasion
traveling long distances on a mule,
his burlap robe flapping in the raw rain—
chilling his phantom limb,

sometimes just to touch the steepled
flesh of his hands
was enough to send her reeling
into prayer—

Because in the end
he arranged for them
to be buried in the same earth,

some say its night musk
still emanates in the graveyard,

a stifled sob come up for air.

The Fallen Angel

after the photograph by Duane Michaels

She's leaning up in the island of her bed,
knees flung open through her French cut teddy
as if she had expected his arrival

through the huge room's starry window
where the radiator glows,
awakened, like her throat

with the sudden host of his tongue in her mouth.
Naked, he's climbed astride her, pulpy wings
strapped to his back and belted round his belly—

If that's a drawback, well,
that's how he got here, winged it—
through a down draft in the alley

and you take what you get sometimes.
She's up for it anyways, up on her elbows,
her many fingers, gasping fish, replenished

by new waters, *and God, I'd take him*,
whoever he is—Zeus, Apollo, Hermes—
gold ringletted hair, maple tree of a torso,

left hand, a wand, casting a spell across her nipple—
But what do I know from sex? It's been a while.
Are angels safe?

Can that plaid woolen blanket maintain
room temperature beneath their weight?
Or will it steam and hydroplane like a magic carpet

launching— Watch those falling pillows
tilt the floor
as if some prime mover

ordained a radiant resurrection,
sun coming up, white-out backdrop,
already the eight-foot windows burning.

Her soul is sold,
though dressed in down-home wings, she thinks
he may be an imposter— Still,

Manhattan slumbers there
suspended like heaven
and his webbed fingers probe

the dimple in her chin,
propping her sweet face eternally under his
so this moment might never end

though if it does—
she'll have this sky-scraping simian
in the loft of her memory. This horny dream,

this shifty apparition, luciferous
spectre in diaphanous flesh—and yes,
God yes, I'm jealous.

Central Park

It was the right hot to work a sweat into.
The pavement, damp trampoline beneath her Reeboks,
a certain give to it, sponging a little, as tar does
after a full day in the brunt of sun.
I can imagine

what she felt when she first saw them
packed into intersecting sidewalks,
a cage of cobras. Before she could spring
from the universe, a voice in her head
ranting over and over
some Mother's warning she can't make out.

How do you cross a street like a lady?
Is your petticoat showing?
Are your stockings straight?

Although she may have grown ashamed
of her bare white legs, her face
pumped with blood like the heart of a lover—
some naked compulsion made her press on.

But how did they stop her?
And where did their hands first touch her?
And was it the hands
first? I can imagine

where she went when she was lifted mercifully
from the torn tissue of her body,
some place where the tortured go
when they no longer sustain pain.
Synapses snap. The bulb on its cord

burns out. Then the slow grown cocoon of coma,
a liminal dream—something like swimming
in a green mesmerizing
downpour of rain.

I'd like to think it was warm and safe
for that single moment—a hammock

of quilted fabric suspended
like the future's wing

before her awakening
into an underworld like no other

where the inhuman imprint,
that huge purple bruise
glared like the wrath of a scorned god.

The Scream

—after the woodcut by Edvard Munch

The sky leaks it first.
Then we're pulled to the oily drift
of the bridge to see where it ends,

if it ends. Pulled
to the figure in the foreground
both less and more than human

holding forever in his hands
both his ears
in a view that will never be over—

so infinite is it.
One raining pitch, a twisted
splicing of lines, clogged—

both less and more
in the pipes of the sky
than the dim canals of the ears.

How it bends and winds
the continuing
etched pen and ink, drilling

the runnels of rough
and worn wooden slats
underneath

with the depth of enduring
inception, luring us
further and further in

to the silent camp of the deaf
where the railing of inner liquids
runs in elliptical rivulets—

transfusions
embalming the brain,
pumping a skeletal premonition

through the facial bones of this gnome
whose hands, upon staring,
become two pinned wings, two

symmetrical slabs of marble
framing the face
like the hair of a woman

so that now it is lion,
serpent, bird—
the shared eye and ear

of the inhuman, wild
with the nightmare,
sustained

in the shadowed
couple
arm in arm

in the tiny background—
calm as the cloud of lake
while ribs of sky

quietly starve
in testament to the steeple
riding its fading spine

to the edge of the cliff,
gliding and ringing
both beneath

and above the bridge,
singing and singing
a gorgon's lullaby.

Billie's Blues

The lies they told her: white slender twelve inch tapers.
Her body trumpeting, scraping its hooves like a trained steed.
My boyfriend bucks the TV, my bedroom's blue walls, wanting
the first drink of the evening and I've left out a long stem wine glass,
empty as any open woman. The tray with a red Cabernet awaits him
in the kitchen. History of germinal jazz on the public station,
Lady in a white camellia—blues. Some ex-lover blackened her spoons,
twisted the tourniquet around the bruises of her arm, slurred words
like curses of a vulture interrupted at his flesh, then two
breast-shaped teardrops moan in a minor key— Full, frontal, flat
paper face of her swaying one-way conversation and I call something
irreverent through the bottle of the hallway. *Whose tears
in the aftermath? Whose unrequited soap opera is this anyway?
Whose hour? Hers? Ours?*

I've an ache just above the palace of my rib-cage
and her white bodice is lace, sutured with pearls,
heavy as a schoolroom window strung with doilies—
She sings. She laments. She struts. Exhale on the up-pull,
inhale on the count, *lean into the resistance* I tell myself,
pumping abdominal crunches on the heirloom oriental and oh,
the backhanded energy of dendrite activity imploding in the adrenal
    glands
like a volcano of panicked sadness or the act of love.

Awaiting Dionysus

Ariadne awoke as the sun spilled
over the east wing of the island.
She stretched and reached for him
in the roomy bed.
But Theseus had left her,
the ball of thread
tied to her heart like a block of ice.
Stone in her throat, swollen moon
that refuses to fade with sunrise.
She swallows it over and over.
She walks the beach.

Her face in the shell-shaped mirror is whiter
and thinner, more blemished and freckled,
older than she remembered.
What did he dread in her deep-set eyes?
The bleached waste of the ocean's bottom?
Debt of treachery to her father
and beast of a brother?
Or was it the reckless liquor of her heights?
The mind that could slice through the labyrinth
breathing passion with manic foresight?

What did he run from?
What claws in her nest of privates?
Was it the mire of her odor after love?

Did he tire of her
inattentive sighs, evenings, her Chopin,
the nocturne in E flat which always moved her
to pour the cognac and stare through the picture

window into the black sky— Gravity of stars
drawing her to her own thoughts.
Was it the fact that she had her thoughts?
Was it the sway and stemming of those thoughts
like the waves' repetitions that washed him away?

Or was he like her brother, a bull at heart,
snorting for new conquests, larger breasts,
firmer ass, tighter dress— *What did he want?*

Never mind. Never mind.
She stirs tea, chops an onion, arranges
beach glass in the ash tray to catch what's left
of morning light.

Frozen moon. Frozen chest.
Frozen heart only a God of Ecstasy
with a killer's rod could release

clasping and pumping the splashy
yeast of the red aorta—

her aftershocks
like lightning in his bare hands.

I Dream The Passion of Emily

after The Master Letters

In the museum
under a great basilica—
the crucifixion
of Emily Dickinson.

I lift her off
her alabaster cross,
an image of the Church's 13th Station.

Holding the small-boned wren
of her body in my arms,
we form a pale Pieta.

Through a hole
in her white dress,
where the evidence of the spear would be,
my fingers find the wound
of Master's *tomahawk.*

And I know *white sustenance,* know
what was sacrificed

for the poems tied
in fascicles, disinterred
from the father's house.

I lift her fallen hand
read the palm,
infinity's pencil,
promise of circumference

yet to come. Loose,
beneath her bridal veil,
the sherry-colored hair
overruns the crown
of buttercups and daisies.

Her heart *is set*
to the lower left,
just like she said—

a full moon
folding to a crescent.

But the love is the same.

The Rump of Honor

The Iliad, *Book VI*

Outside the noisy wailing of the women in the kitchen,
sinister recognitions burdening her tongue,
Andromache holds her baby close,
moans softly to herself.

She eyes the gold corona of the sunset in the archway,
Persian curtains drawn, sienna light from the oval window
casting shadow on the stone steps of the stairway
to the palace lookout. She moves up, and up,
and finally out onto the cobbled deck and ramp,
overlooking the faint lights of fires in the distance.

Soon her dashing warrior hustles up beside her
while little Astynax, shifting in the blanket of her arms,
shakes the one year of his life in his tiny fists.
He's startled to see Hector, his father's spiked helmet,
plumes bobbing as if taunting him. Frightened,
he screeches like a cormorant.

But Andromache smiles
despite Hector's grotesque silhouette
thrown from the turret lantern's flare
and when he tosses off his headgear, quills falling
like applause, his young son sees

this is Papa—and all three begin to laugh—
not knowing this will be their last unified moment.
The shrill wind pins the muscles of their grins.

Then, intuiting the shipwrecked sobbing
of her heart, she pleads with Hector not to fight,
while he swears after the slaughter
he will bring the rump of honor on a platter

ensconced in grapes as green as emeralds, pomegranates
polished as rose quartz, and pears gone topaz
like his armour under the midday sun—

But Andromache's heard enough— *Goddamn him
and goddamn the dead Patrocolus!*

Couldn't he see the camps of Argos, Achilles' wrath
radiating from his tent, the harbor with its eerie
chartreuse fluorescence? Couldn't he picture Zeus's
dipping scales, spears angled for the doomed Troy?

Hector only looks at his little boy. *I hope he lives
to kill the men that kill his father*

he says, blessing the child
with a series of heroic swirls,

cushioning the air
to the last path
little Astynax would travel
off the high walls

where the invading soldiers hurled him,
cheering as he fell.

Demeter, Later

I think she understood the loom
of that particular veil too well,
the dicey riches he pulled her down into,
intimate mist off the river, figments
of figures she might never have recognized
in the upper world. I denied those ruins

but Hades' hands were blue, shady
with passion fruit and when Persephone
saw color, how could she refuse
its complement, aeolian voices
through the fog, tall ships
of beautiful grief. All through childhood

she chose to withdraw to the west rooms of the Kingdom,
overlooking water, irreversible clouds, time,
submerged in its small stall of forgivenesses,
tugging at her sandals like a dog.

I know the longer she reigns
on that jeweled throne adjacent to his,
her ties to my arms will diminish like hunger,
like a starving body eats itself—empty
reflection in the mirrors of Dis.

My breath taps like an icy finger. I'll kill
the green world till her next intermission.
Other gods say it's six of one, it's even…
but she's grown partisan to his spirit, the skull
of his heart. I'll splinter windows

each winter with frost, slam
my icicle vulnerability, though more and more
I see I've lost the frilled possibilities
of a daughter like I've forgotten
blonde meadows under summer's ascension
or the gargantuan dignity of leafed trees.

Instead I've come to know sorcery
in this dark monarch and his lady,

their underworld coupling,
pleasure and disaster
made for each other.

The Physicist's Wife

Just Ten

Like a princess at the dressing table,
I rolled Mother's golden hairbrush
into my long, uncombed
straight hair.

I twirled it tight as a scroll
to hold court there
on the right side of my head.

I hairsprayed it as much as I could
until the ozone in the room broke down
and I was sick in the nostrils
wearing this full-blown crown
in my hair. Hours later

we still couldn't get it out.
Bristles had sewn into my scalp
like a toenail that keeps growing
after death.

My eyes teared as Mother held her breath
and pried that stubborn laureate,
the slats of hair like frozen fur,
a matted animal in a trap—

It was a strange fright
the mirror shot back,
the failed scheme of becoming beautiful
in one graceful sweep of easy curl.

Mother cut the hairbrush out,
my hair shorn to a poor boy's cut,
the severed ends tied in the brush
like some polluted clump we fished
from the pond at Girl Scout Camp.

I was just ten
in my new feminine regret
that vanity could coax me
into what I didn't want.

The Adolescent

That day in the field—did I imagine it?
Did the sixteen year old neighbor
flash me the pornographic pin-up
he'd torn from a tack in my uncle's shed?

I had never seen nipples so erect, netted legs spread,
hands propped behind a head of red hair—
I think I gasped.

I think I felt a warm purring
in the ducts of my own new breasts.

As the light flexed over the spacious acreage,
I think a breeze minced the air
to the sound of held breath
so the corn stalks seemed to pulse and contract,
spreading their silk like stockings of nasty gossip.

My younger cousin doesn't remember but I swear
she lay slouched on a stack of tires drinking
a rootbeer she wouldn't share. She didn't see me
slapped by the pin-up and I was glad. But the boy knew

how later, alone, I'd strip myself bare on an iron bed
in a locked room at the far end of my grandparents'
farmhouse, twisting my torso and long legs
into the damage of that pose.

The Physicist's Wife

August 1945: that small town where my parents lived.
That poor town out west, a city of cancer since
the experiments blasted the cactus out of the desert ground.

A young doctor, my father, cleansed burns and did skin grafts
on anonymous subjects. *Top secret.*
Under the auspices of the government, he was not allowed questions.
Yet he and my mother, my beautiful mother, like a young
    Eva Gabor—
made friends with their neighbors, physicians
and scientists, not by coincidence— But I'm telling the story
of the physicist's wife, who, at that time

in all of their lives, in that wilderness
of government housing, one steamy night
at one of my parents' rowdy patio parties,
after too much gin fizz, tore off her red dress
and threw it off the embankment into the unkempt current

of the Columbia River. Though the undertow was black and thick,
the dress skimmed the surface and floated
like some discarded costume of Esther Williams, swelling
as if coated with toxins, as if certain of its own
sudden and violent death and struggled against it—

while Mrs. Physicist, strolling back up the lawn in her slip,
approached the hors d'oeuvres, indifferent to both food
and liquor until she saw the hot pepper and mushroom arrangement
and stared, terrified and transfixed, as if recognizing premonition.

My mother, back in her kitchen, playing the perfect hostess
looked up and in her distraction
grabbed the wrong glass from her cardboard cupboard
to pour maple syrup all over the huge Caesar Salad.

Everyone slurped the last ice cubes from Old Fashions
and Whiskey Sours, began to devour the barbecued steaks,
to ravage the sweetened lettuce, redness of bursting tomatoes,
sappy flesh of anchovies— The whole party now drunk
on the mystery ingredient in the dressing and my mother

never confessing as the guests raved *simply delicious*—
while off to one side of the sun-dried garden,
picking the snapdragons and madly gathering wild begonias

was the physicist's wife, eye make-up flowing
in tears down her neck, ruining her slip, staining
delicate skin at the V of her breasts

as she stood alone, anguished, unnoticed and half-undressed.

All this— Just hours
before Hiroshima was hit.

Rainmakers

The sheets peel off like gauze.
I kick both feet, you fling your arms.
We lie here with nothing on but sweat
and streaks of moonlight. By midnight

we begin to plot, pack the fan with ice,
breathe back something else besides
each other's smoky eyes, whispers
like divination rods
dousing air for storm.

Humidity surrounds us. We baah like sheep
in their thick hummus of wool.
And yet these bleats can't cool
or fill the deflated heart: each half
smacked inside-out by salt, drought,

evaporation. Thank the Lord
we're living near the sea!
Somewhere inland there's a sapling
clenching fleshy roots, sucking
moisture from the cracked land.

Somewhere else the sky in our names
burns off like fog. Not to mention ducts
of moons that flood the planets.
We're all victims when it comes
to the same dry facts, heat
and wild elements. It's the weeds

that sing off-key, the way my throat
constricts and wilts when I want
to call you *darling*, when I want
to baste your skin with the velouté
of my own baked body. Clouds

of TV blue lift the room like helium
while half-consciously my knee
feels for your thigh. That's
when Lancaster says to Hepburn

You gotta take my deal
because it's gonna be a hot night.
And the world goes crazy on a hot night.

The Tanning Salon

You climb into the lighted coffin,
close the lid, drift
through the white noise,
the nose-cone of a rocket

until countdown ends
and fluorescence pours
over your open pores
sealing the oily coat of melanin

stimulators which seep
through the stratum basal
where pigment cells scatter
and the yeasty batter of

epidermis prepares
to radiate interface
between your pasty shell
and that of the outer worlds.

Maybe you could toughen up, after all,
since the skin and the nervous tissue

have the same root cell and while

the sheath of your ego coppers
under the unquestionably
cancerous apparatus,

blood vessels blush
like poppy pods in opium fields.

You surface toasted
and exit naked—
an illuminated animal
behind a new shield, the glow
of an inner mirror
both permeable and cracking

like any good snakeskin.

Jamaica

From the jet's first glide down
like a silver heron
onto primary color and warm wind—

calypso women in embroidered blouses
serenade us through the long line of customs.

We exchange our money for a humid rainbow
of tropical dollars, and rush an unmarked cab—

past the whale snorts of buses,
the shallow aqua inlets, iridescence
thrown off scales of harlequin bass.

Past kiosks of akee fruit and saltfish,
kneeberrie and kiwi pear— Past acres of orchard
and scrappy pasture till we graze
the flowered base of mountains,

thatched shacks like corrugated
doll houses with televisions blaring
amid the waft of fruity garbage from the neighbors.

I want to lie down
on the raft of easy dialect and sway
through the tourmaline vowels of variegated reggae—
sway in the pulse of maracas or drums
of the ultra-violet sun, sway

like breath on the stucco deck of the beach
where a lady from a town called Anchovie
hustles to braid and bead our hair—

I want to lie down on the dreadlocks
of her name, *Ivy Clover,*
to surrender in the bird-like
patois—

No wonder tourism swoons
into this sinuous sashay,
this cornucopia of apricots and coral sand—

while tangerines and kumquats
reflect an Eden afternoon, the rum
with lemon, rum with ice-cream,
rum with ceiling fans and ocean broth—

Unsteady on my feet, liquid in lotion
after a week, I ask—

Is it me slurring this blonde tonic of banana?
Is it me waving this lush hibiscus in my teeth?
I want to lie down with the wild

bouquet of the full-fronded
flesh-red anthurium.

Cold Sore

A bit of rosy leprosy on the upper lip.
The kiss of a tropical sun, that
overzealous lover, your burgeoning religion.
It reminds you—you're still a sinner
as you wonder from under which cloud it's come.

Stress—that itchy sweater of denial
going viral when the grapevine leaks
the man who broke your heart's getting
married! Now that bacteria twitches
with little white blisters—
you have the venom of memory
to blame. Freckled and tan

as a bride in your mirror, you stare
at the cramp of your smile.
And under the altar of frizzed hair,
eyes, seriously blue
as any vow you might want to exchange.

Better the sturdy leather of the skin,
the sizzling lip that can kiss
off a ceremony of dormant pain
under a patchwork of burning
cream. Better the surface
of a face flecked with scars—
than the grape of the heart,
deep and delicate.

The Future That Brought Her Here

—the invisible pressure of some other time on time.
—Ann Lauterbach

She's still discovering injury.
The childhood doll
with its cobalt eyes struck open,
ginger lashes greasy with years,
a death in her retina
where only an absence appears.

The woman blinks
into the dawning, violet
light of her bedroom
rinsed in hallucination—

Wrapped in the quilt
of her flowering sorrow,
she arranges the cumulative rain.

Birds swoop and crop her terrain
in a scree of time
and the room slides through its layered history:

bookcase into fireplace,
latex into lacy paper,
the same hydrangeas bluing the air.

And she is years back, masked
to an earlier sensation, married

to memory that blunts her senses
the way hunters' headlights stun
deer. And she falls

through the future
that brought her here.

The Furthest Point

Last week when the whales swam sideways
hurling whitecaps through our harbor,
zoologists speculated with each dive
how close to the beaching they were—
A natural suicide, funereal procession.
Diseased, we also dangle here

at the furthest point northeast
where the Atlantic pulls us backward
like a dancer steeped in nostalgia
for a frozen pose. A purple shawl
drapes the boughs of her shoulders
like a wound she won't allow to close.

Evenings like this I wish I had no memory,
then I could roam the dense fathoms of the city
collecting *everything* freshly, dresses laced with dulse,
coral-colored scarves. I could scavenge
as for shells, the faces of new lovers—
what we take for granted is never truly ours.

But this is the beauty, the sadness of the world
here in this small New England city.
My face like a lone bell in some abandoned
clapboard chapel. You

anonymously lighting a cigarette,
side-stepping people as you cross traffic
while each stranger passes holding,
in the bundle of his coat, a heart
wrapped in butcher's paper
like red meat.
Sweet hearts. *Sweetheart*—

⌐∽

The islanders hurry past my doorway
lugging knapsacks filled with groceries, bags
from L.L. Bean. A few might miss the ferry,
come in to browse off-shore a minute. I believe,
at certain times, we can't help be but what we feel—

while around the piers a lost whale
bobs a moment to the unfamiliar
surface of Casco Bay.

Let's not ask each other anything.
We're breathing under separate tanks of oxygen—
like winter lobstermen who never learn to swim,
we take the risk of freezing
or being saved.

Accidental Heart

Interlude

I'm always home now. It's what I do.
Think. No, muse. Ride the shuttle of my daze
between the kitchen and the garden,
await the buds of an epoch's revelations,

brood like the blue delphiniums in perennial
impatience. I close my eyes and rinse my sleep—

all capes and boots, beach roses, caves
and islands—blue speculums to detect disease
and estranged relations. Reasons I won't answer the phone.
I like to sit in the sparse darkness of daylight saved
as April floats its dulse aroma through both hours of afternoon
when I can leave the window open, cajole the foghorns
into weeping their eclipse of veil onto my hair.

Today I drink rainwater with my red pepper sandwich
while recording the coded songs of gulls.
I fold the Lebanese bread, lick the melting snow of mayo,
chew and sketch the silver scrolls of muscular staff,
all b flats and g minors, one liners
out of context—an emotional braille
I can sing alone and never understand.

Sky moving gullscript, elusive swells
defying a tune— Red peppers and pomegranates
daring the earth to make room
for the Venusian explosion,

while dreams run
the off-schedule metro
from memory to prophecy.

Where I Was

...*knowing the world begins from where we are.*
—Richard Jackson

That morning I left for Maine, I left you
a note and drove through the painful yellow sunshine
a little recklessly, wanting so to reach the shaded mountains
before the day got too drunk on its own merciless heat.
From the spiraling asphalt of the Kangamangus
already an hour out of Vermont, still high,
I couldn't relax until I'd crossed the line
into another state. From where I was then, already
too far to turn back, it would begin, that long unraveling
whereby the mind and heart would find each other out.
You were where you were, asleep or occupied, and I

could clear the bleary finger-paint of my last doubt,
focus events to calcify before you even read the note.
I wanted to say what I never wrote, just to put those
words to sleep. I needed to rock past the sudden signs
for Scenic Views the forest delivers up unexpectedly
after each hairpin turn. Up there my ears were dulled
with the still insistent hum of midsummer
as if the air rang its glow inside the warning
of that light. Miles of moments passing sang
beneath the tragic aria my tape was playing
like geography erasing beneath the windows of a plane.

A person needs those sensations, those transitions,
that is, a person needs to know the truth about the way
the world lives, how it goes on inhumanly indifferent
to the common onslaught of impossible love.
At one o'clock I stopped and parked near a shallow stream
that rushed over lime-green stones so effortlessly
I felt confident I could wade, never step in the same
spot twice. That was the water of where I was
and where you were was gone— *I hate goodbyes,*
hated the beautiful dapple of that forest light,
that sun spangling through the cool trees.

Beneath that gold piece, I yielded memory,
watching everything compartmentalized by the mind
while the heart never grows any wiser, never knows

its own capacity for nonsense or longing and lies
like a burnt star and divides what we feel. Tonight I feel
that star is open inside my body. My body that will lie
down on the edge of a coast five hours east of you
and listen to the soft host of a summer wind while
your body will rest inland in that valley of small solace
I drove up out of, that blue valley where grasses lull
as they hold you in their cupped hands.

Toward The Red Moon

...language is grasp, not what we grope for.
—*William Bronk*

As if the liquidity of the moment
reinforced the past
and you were forced to live
in the cut crystal of memory,
each facet meant to multiply
the splay of shattered light
and to continue.

As if each dancing city of your mind
would solidify
into a prism
and thereby rinse its dance
in a lightshow
of opposing effects

like a mirror image that lies
in the projections of inverted rooms—

The right hand on the left brow
where the migraine implodes
into the source of its own sore

dripping impressions
on the sponge in the bathroom sink,
the leaky faucet that erodes dreams.

If only the right hand
could lever her outpour
so that when you awoke
you would go to your desk
where the breakers unfolded
into words that meant more

than the shore they lapped.
And you would catch the fading
blue orchid of a phrase
that bled like a blackened ice-wall

in sudden thaw—and while the loose dark
coursed from your room
in the obvious direction of the boathouse,
the boat glowed
over the kerosene of a raving
ocean—then, only then

would your arms open
to embrace the fiery path
of new white stars

over the contours of the right brain
toward the high sands, toward the red moon.

Inside This Miracle

This morning's dream: three deer
flying. The wingless leader
wears a Sagittarian arrow shaved
into the mauve felt of her snout

like the lines hairdressers cut
into the short coifs of punks,
a signature style—but what
does she want to tell me?

Like Diana, The Huntress, I have my hounds?
Or is she simply the mutable fire of Self,
a protean burning?

No matter. I love her.
She and her two ringing cronies
as they lift into formation, high
on the blue vodka of an August sky

while I stand below on an aisle of beach,
winnowed brow of a world I know only
from inside this miracle.

I want to press my cheek to hers
but there's glass between us
and the light inside it says
warm, says *fragile*, says
not yet yours.

So I can kiss only this shield
with the fishy smudge of a child's
spread-eagled lips
squashed against a car window,

my mouth, shoved moist, wants to imprint
a tattoo of pink flesh like the arrow
which marks her profile.

But she's undaunted
by the wet petals of my wish
and bears down on the cuffs of her hooves

leaping from view
to follow her arrow—

until the air itself heats
and speeds up.

Self-Portrait In August: Letter To An Analyst

Listen— I miss you
even though I owe you money—stuck in the stale
trill of my heart, ticking through summer,
tramping the beach at twilight, while the water
canters away from me on its dark hooves.
Introspecting into the coiled depths of a shell,
I want, I want and there's no one to tell this to,

no one here to interpret my dream: my brother
reproducing Van Gogh's paintings as his own
and the gallery opening in a post-modern wing
jutting off our childhood home.

There's Kirk Douglas's desperation in his face
from the movie Lust For Life, my own
disease and only association— And tonight

the almanac says there's a Green Corn Moon—a reaper
I watch inflate and breaststroke on the ocean.

⤳

In the dream the critics thought my brother crazy
and I kept finding under archways
more fragrant roomfuls of art—

Yellow fields of corn, wind like whizzing stars,
sunflowers, stark and gawking. The shimmer on Auvers' stairs,
the ascetic bed at Arles, shadows like gallows locking
asylum halls at Saint Remy—irises in black
organza dresses, heather, nettles, Van Gogh's boots
crouching like rats along the Charles.

I try to imagine
how you'd walk me through each scene,
how it would feel to be the supposed
artist of all this beauty,

to live off my brother's money,
to argue technique with Gauguin,
believe what the wheat said,

gnaw at my ear with a dull razor
and send it away. *Listen,*

I don't care whose money it is
or if he's a fraud—
I'm intimate with the voices
and I'd cut this moon out of my window
and mail it to you
if I thought it would keep them quiet—

if I thought I could rocket off my chaos
into a meteor shower's fire

which Van Gogh might sizzle and stir
the night before the morning he lies
in the endless field,
left hand on a lead revolver

to deepen forever
the spattering hue of his red hair.

⤺

I'm not suicidal. I remember the story, that's all.
He wasn't happy, sold one painting in all his life,
overexposed himself to the southern light,
then went balmy. Some say he ate the paint
and when lead tainted his system,
that was that. Imagine

ingesting those florescent blues!
Flooding chartreuses and crimsons
mixed with his blood
till his brain was a magma palette.

Still another story claims a clanging
in his ear as if God were a hammer
implanting a nail in a drilled metallic language. *God,*

God, I only want summer to stay its waning—
this moon full, this tide, high and wild,
and you—

I want to see your hands, how your fingers move
when you close your eyes.

↜

When I enter the dream again
I'm on both familiar and foreign ground,
my inner brother *is* crazy
and the critics are vicious—I know them well!

I must be at least ten people, so many rooms
in the wings I never knew existed, rooms of olives
and almond blossoms, self-portraits, crows
in hysterical skies—so many twisted

vineyards, sighing cypresses
which weave and bend then look
away, refusing to watch him die.

I Write to Write You

> It is time the stone made an effort to flower.
> Time unrest had a beating heart.
> It is time it were time.
> It is time.
>
> —Paul Celan

I write to write you I'm writing
again. Scanning words whose wedged meanings
only make sense in the presence
of other words, other wedges.
I'm pressing the soft underbellies of clouds
into abysses where words can't go—

As if anything ever made sense
without physical equivalents.
But sense flies out!
A red-winged eagle from terracotta dust,
and Oh, those fathoms of pregnant canyons—
Then it vanishes in the heavens

like the promise of us
which comprises nothing at all
but its ribboned letters,
its lipsticked oils staining a canvas
of hieroglyphics—*our idea of ourselves*

giving breath and image to thought,
a mantra, recessed, to be lulled
and pampered with the bedrest of something
dreamed, hinted at in the kitchen, early
before birds or the lure of coffee.

It's the memory of memory, fantasy
in the salt-laden hallways of time.
As if the mind were the ocean
that called down the tides
with its one sunset swallow—

When the song that arises
is *because* of the sky's broad, vermillion
arms and the opaque yawn of the morning
that insists while I'm lifting the shades,

it is, indeed, beginning again—still inchoate
but coughing and clearing its throat.

Accidental Heart

The moon invented my sorrow.
Arced it into a small body of prayer
diminishing nothing.
Not the earth with her nervous cities.
Not the shadows holding onto their thin coats.
Not the ocean of woods outside tonight
where there is nothing

but blue snow. My throat opens, then deepens.
My mouth, full of sky, I swallow the lunar
drops. Snow falls on branches inside my chest.
Sometimes an owl peers from the darkness
to embarrass my longing. Still,
I am cloistered in milky light,
a tower of dawn.

Mist rises from my garments.
Morning rises like a flock of nuns.
Soon the moon will lose her translucent
stairway to truth. Far from here
there is pain, excessive heat, people
needing to touch.

The forest is private.
I'll practice resistance in daylight,
folding sorrow deep in my pocket
like an accidental heart.
Compared to the world I am joyful.

Special thanks to
Bobbi Coogan, Martín Espada, Jeffrey Greene, Betsy Kenedy,
Tim Liu, Kenneth Rosen, Betsy Sholl,
Pamela Stewart, David Wojahn and David Williams
for their help, advice and response to these poems in manuscript.

Thanks also to
the MacDowell Colony for a fellowship enabling me
to finalize this manuscript.

Alice James Books has been publishing poetry since 1973. One of the few presses in the country that is run collectively, the cooperative selects manuscripts for publication and the new authors become active members of the press, participating in editorial and production activities. The press was named for Alice James, sister of William and Henry, whose gift for writing was ignored and whose fine journal did not appear until after her death.

Recent Titles:

Rita Gabis, *The Wild Field*
Jeffrey Greene, *To the Left of the Worshiper*
Alice Jones, *The Knot*
Nancy Lagomarsino, *The Secretary Parables*
Timothy Liu, *Vox Angelica*
Margaret Lloyd, *This Particular Earthly Scene*
Suzanne Matson, *Durable Goods*
Jean Valentine, *The River at Wolf*
David Williams, *Traveling Mercies*